D0328300

Mom and Son Journal

Fun, Prompted Journal to Get to Know your Teen Son Better

Catherine Adams

Preface

One morning I woke up to find that my sweet, little adorable boys had somehow transformed into young men full of attitude, hormones, and opinions.

Realizing this, I knew I needed to stop seeing my sons as little children to nurture and love, and start getting to know them as the young adults they had become. This journal is that journey.

My three teen sons and I have gone through this journal together. There were a lot of things left out that I thought were perfect, but they thought were annoying. Through the process, I learned more about them and I felt they actually appreciated me wanting to get to know them better.

I have absolutely no training in psychology or therapy, so please, if you are having serious issues with your son, seek counsel from a professional. The aim of this journal is to have some fun and learn a little more about your amazing son.

Copyright © 2017by Catherine Adams.
All rights reserved. This book or any portion thereof
may not be reproduced or used in any manner whatsoever without
the express written permission of the publisher.

First Printing, 2017
ISBN 978-1544911625

How to use this journal

Take it slow. Teens are quickly annoyed by too many questions! Try to keep it to no more than 2 two pages/questions per day, unless of course, he wants to do more.

Use the journal in the way that makes the most sense for you and your son. If he doesn't like to write, just read the questions to him. If he enjoys writing, then you can take turns filling out the pages. Please remember, the goal is to get to know him a little better, not to fill up pages.

If there are questions that don't apply or that either of you don't like...skip them! If your son only wants to do "the fun pages", that's fine! I guarantee that no matter how few pages you complete, you will learn something new about your son. You can both also modify pages by providing only one response instead of two or three. There are a few blank pages at the end of the journal for you to come up with your own questions if you wish.

I sincerely hope that you will be able to discuss your answers with each other, bond, and above all else, have fun!

My son and I are starting this journal

_____
(date)

My hope is that we will :

_____ have a little fun with it

_____ get to know each other a little better

_____ do a little bonding

_____ _____

I promise never to ask for more than 2 pages a day and I will let him skip any pages he doesn't feel like doing.

_____
(sign)

Son – answer

I have agreed to try this journal because:

_____   my mom asked me to

_____   I appreciate that she wants to
            get to know me better

_____   she bribed me

_____   _____

If we complete at least _____ percent
we will celebrate by:

_____

_____
                (sign)

Your son woke up this morning with one of the following traits. How will he rank which he would want to be?

_____ Stunningly Handsome

_____ Crazy Smart

_____ Super Popular

_____ Wildly Talented

Optional: After you both have answered, discuss or write why you chose the traits you did or if you were surprised by each others choices:

_____

_____

_____

_____

_____

_____

_____

_____

You woke up this morning with one of the following traits. Rank them from 1- 4 which you would want to be:

_____ Stunningly Handsome

_____ Crazy Smart

_____ Super Popular

_____ Wildly Talented

Optional: After you both have answered, discuss or write why you chose the traits you did or if you were surprised by each others choices:

_____

_____

_____

_____

_____

_____

_____

_____

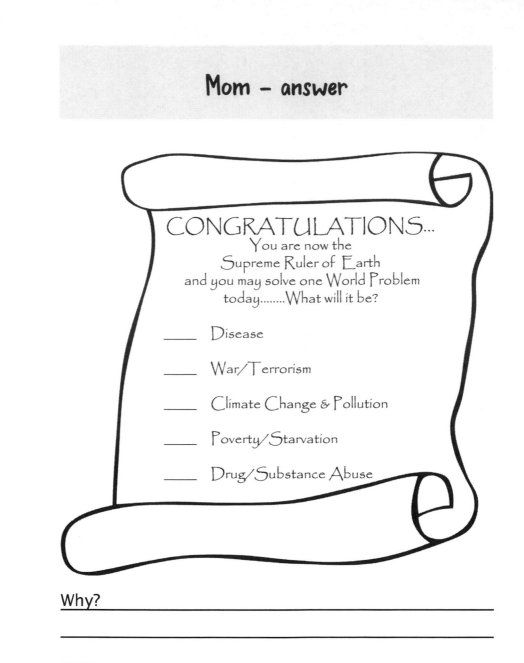

CONGRATULATIONS...
You are now the
Supreme Ruler of Earth
and you may solve one World Problem
today........What will it be?

_____ Disease

_____ War/Terrorism

_____ Climate Change & Pollution

_____ Poverty/Starvation

_____ Drug/Substance Abuse

Why? _____
_____
_____
_____
_____
_____

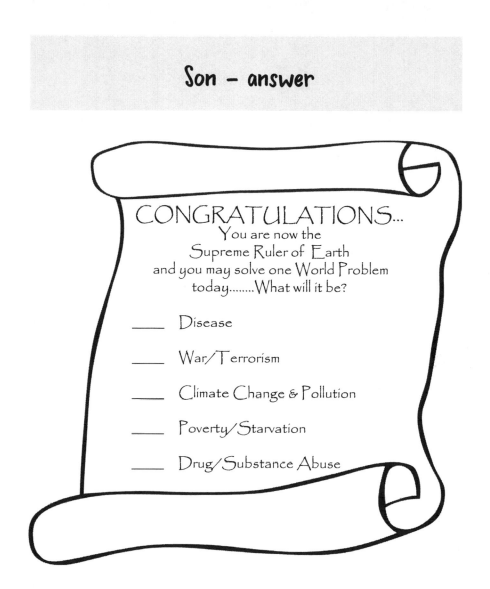

CONGRATULATIONS...
You are now the
Supreme Ruler of Earth
and you may solve one World Problem
today........What will it be?

_____ Disease

_____ War/Terrorism

_____ Climate Change & Pollution

_____ Poverty/Starvation

_____ Drug/Substance Abuse

Why? _____

_____

_____

_____

_____

_____

_____

When you were little where was the scariest place in your room?

_____   Under the bed

_____   In the closet

_____   Outside the window

_____   Somewhere else?

What did you think was hiding? What did you think would happen? (write/share/discuss)

_____

_____

_____

_____

_____

_____

_____

_____

When you were little where was the scariest place in your room?

_____   Under the bed

_____   In the closet

_____   Outside the window

_____   Somewhere else?

What did you think was hiding? What did you think would happen? (write/share/discuss)

_____

_____

_____

_____

_____

_____

_____

_____

Mom – answer

What 2 things are you the most worried about regarding your son right now?

_____

_____

What 2 things are you the most worried about regarding your son in the future?

_____

_____

Optional: After you both have answered, discuss or write why you chose your answers or if you were surprised by each others choices:

_____

_____

_____

_____

_____

_____

_____

What 2 things are you the most worried about right now?

_____

_____

What 2 things are you the most worried about in the future?

_____

_____

Optional: After you both have answered, discuss or write why you chose your answers or if you were surprised by each others choices:

_____

_____

_____

_____

_____

_____

_____

Mom – answer first

About School....
This year what subject does your son...

do the best in?

_____

like the most?

_____

like the least?

_____

find the easiest?

_____

find the hardest?

_____

Optional: After you both have answered, discuss or write if you were surprised by each others choices:

_____

_____

_____

_____

_____

About School....
This year what subject do you...

do the best in?

_____

like the most?

_____

like the least?

_____

find the easiest?

_____

find the hardest?

_____

Optional: After you both have answered, discuss or write if you were surprised by each others choices:

_____

_____

_____

_____

_____

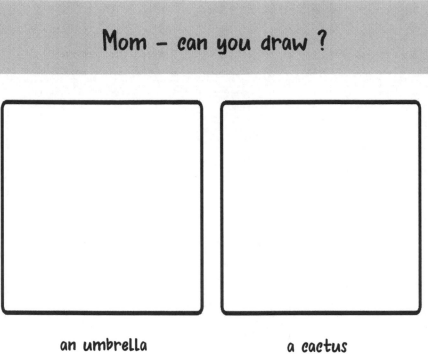

Mom - can you draw ?

an umbrella

a cactus

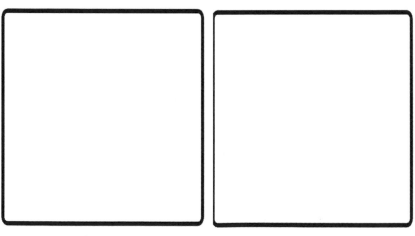

a turtle

a ghost

Son - can you draw ?

an umbrella

a cactus

a turtle

a ghost

Mom - answer first

What are 2 ways you still treat your son like a little kid?

_____

_____

What are two ways you treat him like an adult?

_____

_____

Son – answer

Read what your mom wrote. Check the ones you agree with. If you want to add different things put them below:

_____

_____

_____

_____

CONGRATULATIONS...

You are now a member of one of the following...
Rank your preference and what you think your son will choose.

You   Son

___ Seal Team 6   ___

___ Knights of the
     Round Table   ___

___ Ninjas   ___

CONGRATULATIONS...
You are now a member of one of the following...
Rank your preference:

____ Seal Team 6

____ Knights of the Round Table

____ Ninjas

Mom – answer

What 3 positive traits would describe your son?

What are 2 things he does that you appreciate?

Son – answer

What 2 positive traits would describe your mom?

What is 1 thing she does that you appreciate?

You are stranded on a deserted island for a year so you are stuck with the same meal every day. What would you choose in each food group? (you have water available)

Meat/Protein _____

Carb/Bread/
Rice/Potato _____

Vegetable _____

Drink _____

Dessert _____

You are stranded on a deserted island for a year so you are stuck with the same meal every day. What would you choose in each food group? (you have water available)

Meat/Protein _____

Carb/Bread/
Rice/Potato _____

Vegetable _____

Drink _____

Dessert _____

Mom – answer

List 2 fun things you think your son should do more of:

_____

_____

List 2 fun things you should do more of:

_____

_____

Write about a special memory of something you did together? (write/share/discuss)

_____

_____

_____

_____

_____

_____

_____

_____

_____

Son – answer

List 2 fun things you think your mom should do more of:

_____

_____

List 2 fun things you should do more of:

_____

_____

Write about a special memory of something you did together? (write/share/discuss)

_____
_____
_____
_____
_____
_____
_____
_____

YAY !!!
You just won a tattoo !!!
Are you happy or not?
(circle one)

What is it and where is it going?
(draw or write below)

YAY !!!
You just won a tattoo !!!
Are you happy or not?
(circle one)

What is it and where is it going?
(draw or write below)

Mom – answer

List 3 things you are proud of your son for this year:

_____

_____

_____

Optional: After you both have answered, discuss or write why you chose your answers or if you were surprised by each others choices:

_____

_____

_____

_____

_____

_____

_____

_____

Son – answer

List 3 things you are proud of yourself for this year:

_____

_____

_____

Optional: After you both have answered, discuss or write why you chose your answers or if you were surprised by each others choices:

_____

_____

_____

_____

_____

_____

_____

_____

_____

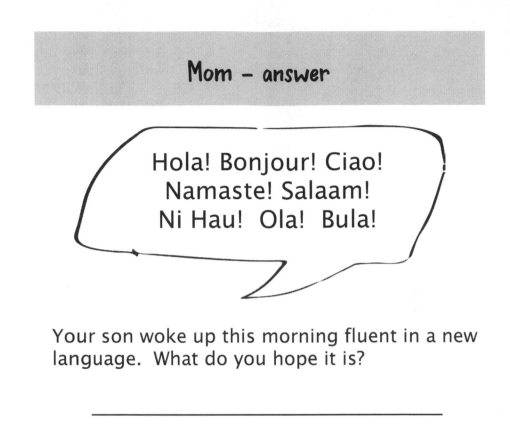

Hola! Bonjour! Ciao!
Namaste! Salaam!
Ni Hau! Ola! Bula!

Your son woke up this morning fluent in a new language. What do you hope it is?

_____

Why?

_____

_____

What would you want it to be for yourself?

_____

Why?

_____

_____

Hola! Bonjour! Ciao!
Namaste! Salaam!
Ni Hau! Ola! Bula!

You woke up this morning fluent in a new language. What do you hope it is?

_____

Why?

_____

_____

What would you want it to be for your mom?

_____

Why?

_____

_____

Mom – answer first

What are 2 things you think you have done right in raising your son?

_____

_____

_____

_____

What is something you wish you had done better or different in raising your son?

_____

_____

_____

_____

What is one thing you could still improve on?

_____

_____

_____

_____

Read what your mom has written.

Place check marks next to the ones you agree with.

Place X's next to the ones you don't agree with.

What is one thing you will do the same in raising your children?

_____

_____

_____

_____

What is one thing you will do different in raising your children?

_____

_____

_____

_____

In your ideal job/career what has been the most important for you? Rank 1-7:

_____ Great location

_____ Rewarding/love it

_____ Lots of travel

_____ High income

_____ Great co-workers

_____ Lots of time off

_____ Makes a difference

Optional: After you both have answered, discuss or write why you chose what you did or if you were surprised by each others choices:

_____

_____

_____

_____

_____

_____

Son – answer first

In your ideal job/career what will be
the most important for you? Rank 1-7:

_____ Great location

_____ Rewarding/love it

_____ Lots of travel

_____ High income

_____ Great co-workers

_____ Lots of time off

_____ Makes a difference

Optional: After you both have answered,
discuss or write why you chose what you did or
if you were surprised by each others choices:

_____

_____

_____

_____

_____

_____

Mom – answer

What are 2 ways men have life easier than women?

_____

_____

What are 2 ways women have life easier than men?

_____

_____

Optional: After you both have answered, discuss or write why you chose what you did or if you were surprised by each others choices:

_____

_____

_____

_____

_____

Son - answer

What are 2 ways men have life easier than women?

_____

_____

What are 2 ways women have life easier than men?

_____

_____

Optional: After you both have answered, discuss or write why you chose what you did or if you were surprised by each others choices:

_____
_____
_____
_____
_____
_____

Mom – answer

Do you believe in miracles? yes / no

Why or why not? (write or discuss)

_____

_____

_____

_____

Do you believe in aliens? yes / no

Why or why not? (write or discuss)

_____

_____

_____

_____

Do you believe in ghosts? yes / no

Why or why not? (write or discuss)

_____

_____

_____

_____

Do you believe in miracles? yes / no

Why or why not? (write or discuss)

_____

_____

_____

_____

Do you believe in aliens? yes / no

Why or why not? (write or discuss)

_____

_____

_____

_____

Do you believe in ghosts? yes / no

Why or why not? (write or discuss)

_____

_____

_____

_____

Mom – answer first

Which will your son think is
better of the choices below?:

	City	Country	
	Kittens	Puppies	
	Marvel	D.C.	
	Vampire	Werewolf	
	Surprises	Planned events	
	Extra Credit	Curve	
	Running	Swimming	
	Winning $20	Finding $20	
	Free appetizer	Free dessert	
	Book smart	Street smart	
	Chocolate	Vanilla	
	Stay up late	Sleep in late	

Which of the choices below is better?

City	Country	
Kittens	Puppies	
Marvel	D.C.	
Vampire	Werewolf	
Surprises	Planned events	
Extra Credit	Curve	
Running	Swimming	
Winning $20	Finding $20	
Free appetizer	Free dessert	
Book smart	Street smart	
Chocolate	Vanilla	
Stay up late	Sleep in late	

Circle the 3 life goals that you wish most for your son:

Being healthy

Having a successful career

Caring for others

Making the world a better place

Finding a life partner

Being rich

Having children

Being happy

Having close friends

Being famous

Exploring/Traveling

Optional: After you both have answered, discuss or write why you chose what you did or if you were surprised by each others choices:

_____

_____

_____

Circle the 3 life goals that you wish most for yourself:

Being healthy

Having a successful career

Caring for others

Making the world a better place

Finding a life partner

Being rich

Having children

Being happy

Having close friends

Being famous

Exploring/Traveling

Optional: After you both have answered, discuss or write why you chose what you did or if you were surprised by each others choices:

_____

_____

_____

Mom – answer

It's the ZOMBIE APOCALYPSE - The only survivors are you and your son!

What three of your son's traits/skills will help you both to survive?

_____

_____

_____

What weapon would he use?

_____

What weapon would you use?

_____

It's the ZOMBIE APOCALYPSE – The only survivors are you and your mom!

What two of your traits/skills will help you both to survive?

_____

_____

What skill would you wish you had?

_____

What weapon would you use?

_____

Check 3 things you'd like to do more of with your son:

_____ cook together

_____ play games

_____ have conversations

_____ be active (walks/bike rides...)

_____ go out to lunch or dinner

_____ go to a movie

_____ play video games

_____ do crafts/art/projects

_____ _____

Optional: After you both have answered, agree to do at least one that you both checked sometime in the next week or two.

_____

_____

_____

Check 3 things you'd like to do more of with your mom:

_____ cook together

_____ play games

_____ have conversations

_____ be active (walks/bike rides...)

_____ go out to lunch or dinner

_____ go to a movie

_____ play video games

_____ do crafts/art/projects

_____ _____

Optional: After you both have answered, agree to do at least one that you both checked sometime in the next week or two.

_____

_____

_____

Mom – answer first

Which 3 qualities do you think your son needs most from you, especially during his teen years?

Encouragement	
Clear and consistent rules	
A sense of humor	
Listening without giving advice	
Genuine interest in activities	
Direction and guidance	
Setting a good example	
Open communication	
Unconditional love	
Understanding and forgiveness	

Optional: After you both have answered, discuss or write why you chose what you did or if you were surprised by each others choices:

_____

_____

_____

_____

_____

Son – answer second

Especially during your teen years, pick the top 2 qualities you need most from your mom:

Encouragement	
Clear and consistent rules	
A sense of humor	
Listening without giving advice	
Genuine interest in activities	
Direction and guidance	
Setting a good example	
Open communication	
Unconditional love	
Understanding and forgiveness	

Optional: After you both have answered, discuss or write why you chose what you did or if you were surprised by each others choices:

_____

_____

_____

_____

_____

In what two ways are you and your son the most alike?

_____

_____

In what two ways are you and your son the most different?

_____

_____

Optional: After you both have answered, discuss or write why you chose what you did or if you were surprised by each others answers:

_____

_____

_____

_____

_____

_____

Son – answer first

In what two ways are you and your mom
the most alike?

_____

_____

In what two ways are you and your mom
the most different?

_____

_____

Optional: After you both have answered,
discuss or write why you chose what you did or
if you were surprised by each others answers:

_____

_____

_____

_____

_____

_____

Mom – answer first

What you say can sometimes be annoying. (hard to believe, I know). Check the ones you say on a regular basis. Check the two you think most annoy your son.

Mom says	say regularly	most annoying
How was school?		
When I was your age...		
Because I said so.		
Are you going to wear that?		
This is why we don't have nice things.		
You're still on that electronic?		
Don't you have any homework?		
You need to clean your room.		
Money doesn't grow on trees.		
You're just going though a phase		
add your own:		

Son – answer second

What your mom says can sometimes be annoying.
Check the ones that you hear on a regular basis.
Check the two that most annoy you.

Mom says	hear regularly	most annoying
How was school?		
When I was your age...		
Because I said so.		
Are you going to wear that?		
This is why we don't have nice things.		
You're still on that electronic?		
Don't you have any homework?		
You need to clean your room.		
Money doesn't grow on trees.		
You're just going through a phase		
add your own:		

Mom – answer

So...it turns out you get a super power on your 50th birthday. What do you hope it is?

_____ mind control

_____ invisibility

_____ super strength

_____ super speed

_____ fly

How will you use it?

_____

_____

_____

_____

After answering..were you surprised by each others choices? How?

_____

_____

_____

_____

So...it turns out you get a super power on your 20th birthday. What do you hope it is?

____ mind control

____ invisibility

____ super strength

____ super speed

____ fly

How will you use it?

_____

_____

_____

_____

After answering..were you surprised by each others choices? How?

_____

_____

_____

_____

Do you believe in karma? yes / no

Why or why not? (write or discuss)

_____

_____

_____

_____

Do you believe in love at first sight? yes / no

Why or why not? (write or discuss)

_____

_____

_____

_____

Do you believe in guardian angels? yes / no

Why or why not? (write or discuss)

_____

_____

_____

_____

Do you believe in karma? yes / no

Why or why not? (write or discuss)

_____

_____

_____

_____

Do you believe in love at first sight? yes / no

Why or why not? (write or discuss)

_____

_____

_____

_____

Do you believe in guardian angels? yes / no

Why or why not? (write or discuss)

_____

_____

_____

_____

Mom – answer

You just won a time travel trip!

Do you want to go:

_____ to the past

_____ to the future

what period of time in the past or how far into the future?

_____

_____

What would you want to see or do?

_____

_____

After answering..were you surprised by each others choices? How?

_____

_____

_____

_____

You just won a time travel trip!

Do you want to go:

_____ to the past

_____ to the future

what period of time in the past or how far into the future?

_____

_____

What would you want to see or do?

_____

_____

After answering..were you surprised by each others choices? How?

_____

_____

_____

_____

Do you think your son has ever...

	yes	no
Eaten a bug?		
Been in a physical fight?		
Been bullied?		
Had a crush?		
Lied about his age?		
Stayed up all night?		
Seen something illegal?		
Sent an email or text by mistake?		
Gone skinny dipping?		
Hid something from you?		
Gotten away with something at school?		
Made a prank phone call?		
Been offered weed?		

When you're both done, check the ones on his side that are correct about you. Only do this if you can both handle the truth!

Do you think your mom has ever...

	yes	no
Eaten a bug?		
Been in a physical fight?		
Been bullied?		
Had a crush?		
Lied about her age?		
Stayed up all night?		
Seen something illegal?		
Sent an email or text by mistake?		
Gone skinny dipping?		
Hid something from you?		
Gotten away with something at school?		
Made a prank phone call?		
Been offered weed?		

When you're both done, check the ones on her side that are correct about you. Only do this if you can both handle the truth!

Mom – answer first

Your son just won a *Vacation Home* that he can use every weekend. The perfect place would be...(check one in each group)

located

_____   on the oceanfront

_____   in the mountains

_____   by a lake

with a great view of the

_____   sunrise

_____   sunset

There would be plenty of

_____   outdoor activities

_____   indoor activities

and lots of

_____   quiet time

_____   parties

You just won a **Vacation Home** that you can use every weekend. The perfect place would be...(check one in each group)

located

_____   on the oceanfront

_____   in the mountains

_____   by a lake

with a great view of the

_____   sunrise

_____   sunset

There would be plenty of

_____   outdoor activities

_____   indoor activities

and lots of

_____   quiet time

_____   parties

Rank these places in the order that you would like to stay in for a month (1=1st choice)...

Rank these places in the order that you would like to stay in for a month (1=1st choice)...

Mom – draw your son's favorite

fast food

sport to play

dessert

animal

Son - draw your mom's favorite

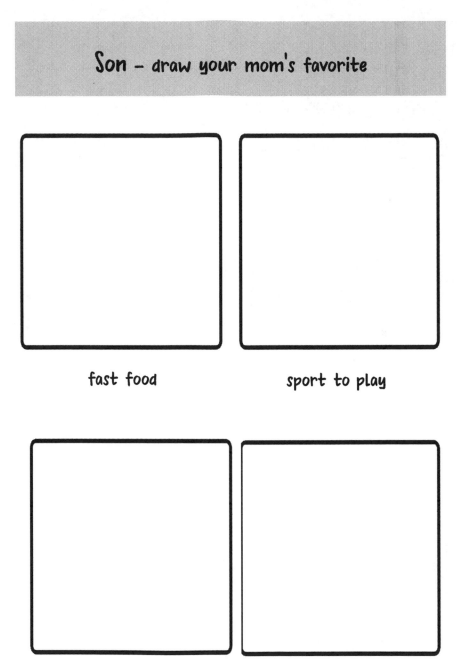

fast food

sport to play

dessert

animal

Check 3 things you hope your son knows:

_____ how much I love him

_____ what a great person I think he is

_____ how much I worry about him

_____ how much I believe in him

_____ how much I trust him

_____ how special he is

_____ how much I expect of him

Check 3 things you hope your mom knows:

_____ that I'm trying

_____ that there are a lot of pressures on me

_____ that I'm not an idiot

_____ that she can trust me

_____ that I'm not going to do anything really stupid

_____ that I need space to grow

_____ that I think about my future

Mom – answer

Question:

_____

_____

_____

Answer:

_____

_____

_____

_____

_____

_____

_____

_____

_____

_____

_____

_____

_____

_____

_____

Son – answer

Question:

_____

_____

_____

Answer:

_____

_____

_____

_____

_____

_____

_____

_____

_____

_____

_____

_____

_____

_____

Mom – answer

Question:

_____

_____

_____

Answer:

_____

_____

_____

_____

_____

_____

_____

_____

_____

_____

_____

_____

_____

_____

_____

_____

_____

Son – answer

Question:

_____

_____

_____

Answer:

_____

_____

_____

_____

_____

_____

_____

_____

_____

_____

_____

_____

_____

_____

_____

_____

Mom – answer

Question:

_____

_____

_____

Answer:

_____

_____

_____

_____

_____

_____

_____

_____

_____

_____

_____

_____

_____

_____

_____

_____

_____

Son – answer

Question:

_____

_____

_____

Answer:

_____

_____

_____

_____

_____

_____

_____

_____

_____

_____

_____

_____

_____

_____

_____

Mom – answer

Question:

_____

_____

_____

Answer:

_____

_____

_____

_____

_____

_____

_____

_____

_____

_____

_____

_____

_____

_____

_____

_____

Son – answer

Question:

_____
_____
_____

Answer:

_____
_____
_____
_____
_____
_____
_____
_____
_____
_____
_____
_____
_____
_____
_____
_____

Mom – answer

Question:

_____

_____

_____

Answer:

_____

_____

_____

_____

_____

_____

_____

_____

_____

_____

_____

_____

_____

_____

_____

_____

_____

Son – answer

Question:

_____

_____

_____

Answer:

_____

_____

_____

_____

_____

_____

_____

_____

_____

_____

_____

_____

_____

_____

_____

_____

Mom – answer

Question:

_____

_____

_____

Answer:

_____

_____

_____

_____

_____

_____

_____

_____

_____

_____

_____

_____

_____

_____

_____

_____

Son – answer

Question:

_____

_____

_____

Answer:

_____

_____

_____

_____

_____

_____

_____

_____

_____

_____

_____

_____

_____

_____

_____

_____

Made in the USA
Middletown, DE
06 March 2020

85931216R00049